I0815505

THE ULTIMATE ANIMAL LIBRARY
Clownfish
by Janie Scheffer
BLASTOFF! READERS
2
BELLWETHER MEDIA • MINNEAPOLIS, MN

Blastoff! Readers are carefully developed by literacy experts to build reading stamina and move students toward fluency by combining standards-based content with developmentally appropriate text.

Level 1 provides the most support through repetition of high-frequency words, light text, predictable sentence patterns, and strong visual support.

Level 2 offers early readers a bit more challenge through varied sentences, increased text load, and text-supportive special features.

Level 3 advances early-fluent readers toward fluency through increased text load, less reliance on photos, advancing concepts, longer sentences, and more complex special features.

★ **Blastoff! Universe**

Reading Level

Grade K

Grades 1–3

Grade 4

This edition first published in 2026 by Bellwether Media, Inc.

Library of Congress Cataloging-in-Publication Data

LC record for Clownfish available at: https://lccn.loc.gov/2025003960

Editor: Elizabeth Neuenfeldt Series Designer: Veah Demmin

Printed in the United States of America, North Mankato, MN.

Table of Contents

What Are Clownfish?

sea anemones

Clownfish are often called anemonefish. They live among **sea anemones**! They live in the Pacific and Indian Oceans.

Common Clownfish Report

Status in the Wild

least concern

Habitats

coral reefs

lagoons

There are around 30 kinds of clownfish. Many are bright orange. Others are yellow, red, or black.

Most of them have white stripes. Sometimes they have dark marks mixed in.

These fish are small.
Many clownfish are around
4 inches (10 centimeters) long.

Females are bigger than males.

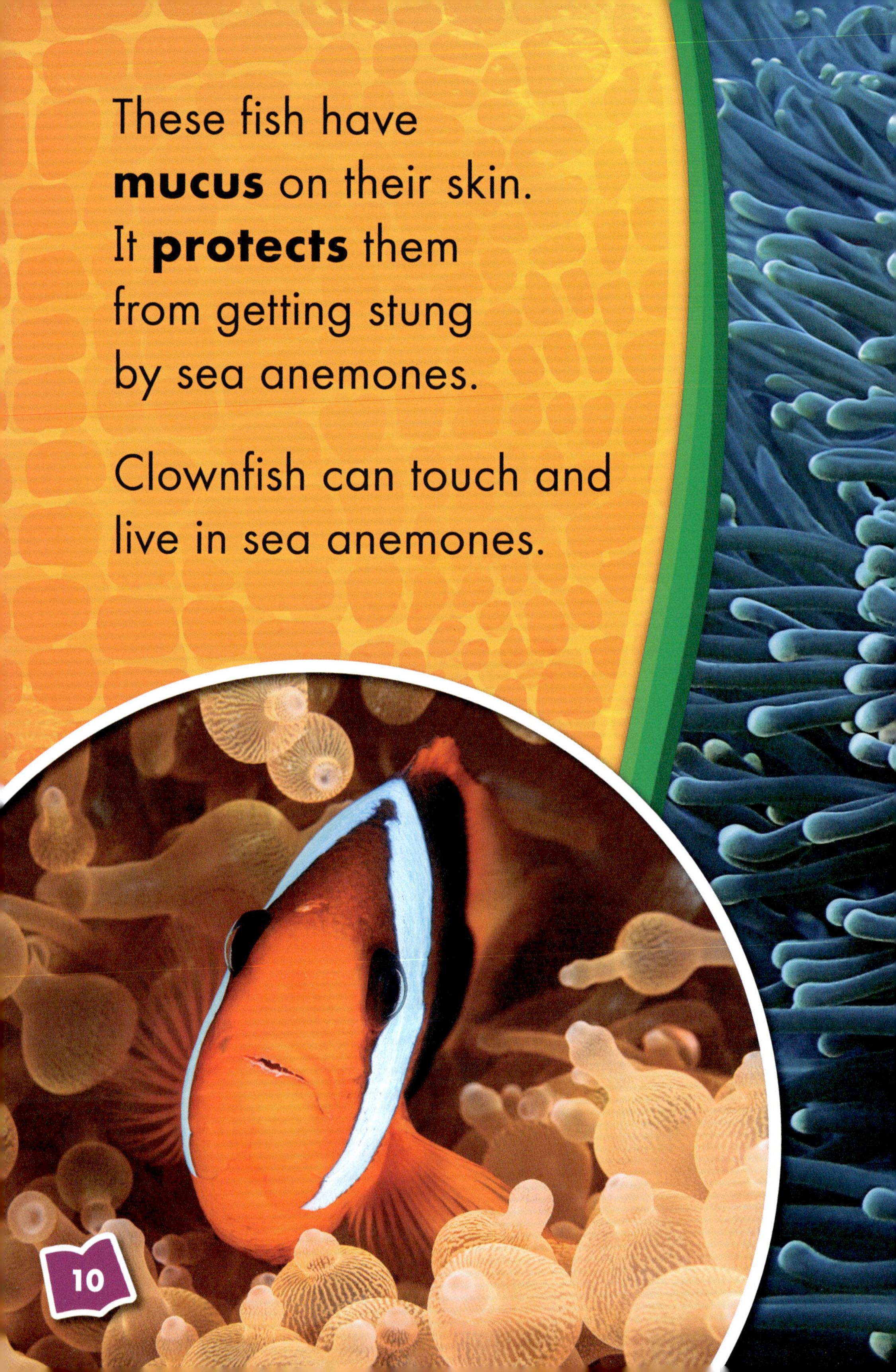

These fish have **mucus** on their skin. It **protects** them from getting stung by sea anemones.

Clownfish can touch and live in sea anemones.

Spot a Clownfish
dark marks
bright orange body
white stripes

Totally Territorial!

Clownfish live in **coral reefs** and **lagoons**. They rest in colorful sea anemones.

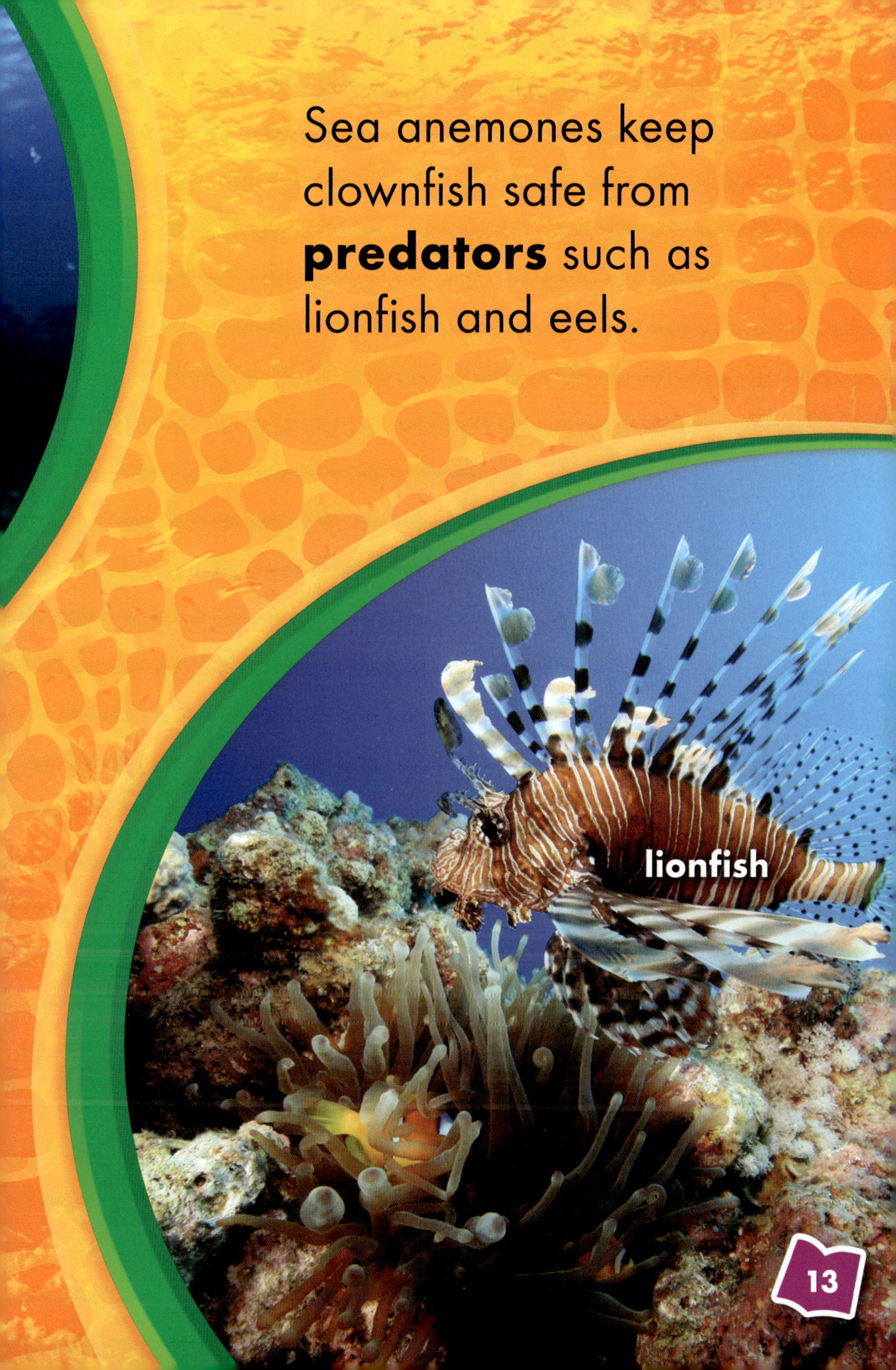

Sea anemones keep clownfish safe from **predators** such as lionfish and eels.

These fish live in small groups.
They are **territorial**.
They stay near their homes.

Clownfish chase away any **intruders**. They protect their anemones from harm.

Clownfish mostly eat **zooplankton**. They also eat **algae**.

At times, they eat food scraps from sea anemones.

Growing Up

Female clownfish can lay thousands of eggs at once. Males protect the eggs.

After about one week, the eggs **hatch**. Baby clownfish come out. They are called **fry**.

eggs

At first, all clownfish are male.
The largest later become female.

Fry are on their own right away. They can live up to 10 years!

Name of Babies

fry

Number of Eggs

thousands

Time Spent in Eggs

Life Span

Glossary

algae—plants and plantlike living things; most kinds of algae grow in water.

coral reefs—groups of corals that grow in warm, shallow ocean waters

fry—baby clownfish

hatch—to break open

intruders—unwanted visitors

lagoons—shallow bodies of water blocked from oceans by coral reefs, atolls, or islands

mucus—a clear liquid that covers the body of a clownfish

predators—animals that hunt other animals for food

protects—keeps safe

sea anemones—small, brightly colored sea animals that look like flowers and stick to rocks and coral

territorial—wanting to keep an area safe

zooplankton—ocean animals that drift in water; most zooplankton are tiny.

To Learn More

AT THE LIBRARY

Riggs, Kate. *Clownfish.* Mankato, Minn.: Creative Education and Creative Paperbacks, 2025.

Sexton, Colleen. *Clownfish.* Minneapolis, Minn.: Kaleidoscope, 2023.

Zimmerman, Adeline J. *Sea Anemones.* Minneapolis, Minn.: Jump!, 2022.

ON THE WEB

FACTSURFER

Factsurfer.com gives you a safe, fun way to find more information.

1. Go to www.factsurfer.com.
2. Enter "clownfish" into the search box and click 🔍.
3. Select your book cover to see a list of related content.

Index

The images in this book are reproduced through the courtesy of: stockpix4u, cover (clownfish); Irina Markova, cover background, interior background; RukiMedia, cover (clownfish icon); Kletr, pp. 3, 17 (clownfish); Karlos Lomsky, p. 4; Sebastien Burel, p. 4 (sea anemones); The Ocean Agency, p. 6; Szancsi, p. 7; Dmitry Rukhlenko, p. 8; Hans Gert Broeder, p. 9; Danita Delimont, p. 10; Josephine Julian, pp. 10-11; Johannes Kornelius, p. 11; whitcomberd, p. 12; Richard Carey, p. 13; Drew, p. 14; Andrei Armiagov, p. 15; treetstreet, pp. 16-17; estionx, p. 17 (eels); bearcreative, p. 17 (lionfish); kichigin19, p. 17 (algae); Joan Carles Juarez, p. 17 (zooplankton); Brook Peterson, p. 18; nori, pp. 18-19; Mike Workman, p. 20; Valeronio, p. 21; bluehand, p. 23.